TO:

_____

FROM:

_____

DATE:

_____

_____

_____

_____

_____

_____

_____

_____

_____

_____

_____

_____

_____

_____

_____

_____

_____

_____

_____

_____

_____

_____

_____

_____

_____

_____

_____

DELIGHT YOURSELF IN THE LORD, AND HE WILL GIVE YOU THE DESIRES OF YOUR HEART.

PSALM 37:4

_____

_____

_____

_____

_____

_____

_____

_____

_____

_____

_____

_____

_____

_____

_____

_____

_____

_____

_____

_____

_____

_____

_____

_____

_____

_____

THE LORD IS MY LIGHT AND MY SALVATION—WHOM SHALL I FEAR?
THE LORD IS THE STRONGHOLD OF MY LIFE—OF WHOM SHALL I BE AFRAID?

PSALM 27:1

THE LORD HIMSELF GOES BEFORE YOU AND WILL BE WITH YOU;
HE WILL NEVER LEAVE YOU NOR FORSAKE YOU.

DEUTERONOMY 31:8

_____

_____

_____

_____

_____

_____

_____

_____

_____

_____

_____

_____

_____

_____

_____

_____

_____

_____

_____

_____

_____

_____

_____

_____

GOD IS WORKING IN YOU, GIVING YOU THE DESIRE TO OBEY HIM AND THE POWER TO DO WHAT PLEASES HIM.

PHILIPPIANS 2:13

_____

_____

_____

_____

_____

_____

_____

_____

_____

_____

_____

_____

_____

_____

_____

_____

_____

_____

_____

_____

_____

_____

I CAN DO EVERYTHING THROUGH CHRIST, WHO GIVES ME STRENGTH.

PHILIPPIANS 4:13

_____

_____

_____

_____

_____

_____

_____

_____

_____

_____

_____

_____

_____

_____

_____

_____

_____

_____

_____

_____

_____

_____

_____

_____

IF YOU WANT TO KNOW WHAT GOD WANTS YOU TO DO, ASK HIM, AND HE WILL GLADLY TELL YOU.

JAMES 1:5

_____

_____

_____

_____

_____

_____

_____

_____

_____

_____

_____

_____

_____

_____

_____

_____

_____

_____

_____

_____

_____

_____

_____

_____

_____

CREATE IN ME A PURE HEART, O GOD, AND RENEW A STEADFAST SPIRIT WITHIN ME.

PSALM 51:10

_____

_____

_____

_____

_____

_____

_____

_____

_____

_____

_____

_____

_____

_____

_____

_____

_____

_____

_____

_____

_____

_____

_____

_____

_____

_____

IF ANYONE IS IN CHRIST, HE IS A NEW CREATION; THE OLD HAS GONE, THE NEW HAS COME!

2 CORINTHIANS 5:17

_____

_____

_____

_____

_____

_____

_____

_____

_____

_____

_____

_____

_____

_____

_____

_____

_____

_____

_____

_____

_____

_____

_____

_____

CAST YOUR CARES ON THE LORD AND HE WILL SUSTAIN YOU.

PSALM 55:22

THE LORD YOUR GOD IS WITH YOU, HE IS MIGHTY TO SAVE. HE WILL TAKE GREAT
DELIGHT IN YOU, HE WILL QUIET YOU WITH HIS LOVE.
ZEPHANIAH 3:17

_____

_____

_____

_____

_____

_____

_____

_____

_____

_____

_____

_____

_____

_____

_____

_____

_____

_____

_____

_____

_____

_____

_____

_____

_____

_____

THE LORD IS FAITHFUL TO ALL HIS PROMISES AND LOVING TOWARD ALL HE HAS MADE.

PSALM 145:13

_____

_____

_____

_____

_____

_____

_____

_____

_____

_____

_____

_____

_____

_____

_____

_____

_____

_____

_____

_____

_____

_____

_____

**IN YOU, O LORD, DO I PUT MY TRUST AND CONFIDENTLY TAKE REFUGE;
LET ME NEVER BE PUT TO SHAME OR CONFUSION!**

PSALM 71:1

_____

_____

_____

_____

_____

_____

_____

_____

_____

_____

_____

_____

_____

_____

_____

_____

_____

_____

_____

_____

_____

_____

_____

_____

_____

"BE STRONG AND COURAGEOUS . . . THE LORD YOUR GOD WILL BE WITH YOU WHEREVER YOU GO."

JOSHUA 1:9

DEPEND ON THE LORD IN WHATEVER YOU DO,
AND YOUR PLANS WILL SUCCEED.

PROVERBS 16:3

_____

_____

_____

_____

_____

_____

_____

_____

_____

_____

_____

_____

_____

_____

_____

_____

_____

_____

_____

_____

_____

_____

SINCE WE HAVE BEEN JUSTIFIED THROUGH FAITH,
WE HAVE PEACE WITH GOD THROUGH OUR LORD JESUS CHRIST.

ROMANS 5:1

THE LORD IS MY ROCK, MY FORTRESS AND MY DELIVERER;
MY GOD IS MY ROCK, IN WHOM I TAKE REFUGE.

PSALM 18:2

_____

_____

_____

_____

_____

_____

_____

_____

_____

_____

_____

_____

_____

_____

_____

_____

_____

_____

_____

_____

_____

_____

_____

_____

"IF ANYONE WOULD COME AFTER ME, HE MUST DENY HIMSELF
AND TAKE UP HIS CROSS AND FOLLOW ME."

MATTHEW 16:24

_____

_____

_____

_____

_____

_____

_____

_____

_____

_____

_____

_____

_____

_____

_____

_____

_____

_____

_____

_____

_____

_____

_____

_____

THE WORD OF THE LORD IS RIGHT AND TRUE; HE IS FAITHFUL IN ALL HE DOES.

PSALM 33:4

_____

_____

_____

_____

_____

_____

_____

_____

_____

_____

_____

_____

_____

_____

_____

_____

_____

_____

_____

_____

_____

_____

_____

_____

THE LORD IS MY STRENGTH, MY SHIELD FROM EVERY DANGER. I TRUST IN HIM WITH ALL MY HEART.

PSALM 28:7

_____

_____

_____

_____

_____

_____

_____

_____

_____

_____

_____

_____

_____

_____

_____

_____

_____

_____

_____

_____

_____

_____

_____

_____

IN HIM WE HAVE REDEMPTION THROUGH HIS BLOOD, THE FORGIVENESS OF
SINS, IN ACCORDANCE WITH THE RICHES OF GOD'S GRACE.

EPHESIANS 1:7

_____

_____

_____

_____

_____

_____

_____

_____

_____

_____

_____

_____

_____

_____

_____

_____

_____

_____

_____

_____

_____

_____

_____

_____

I TRUST IN YOUR UNFAILING LOVE. I WILL REJOICE BECAUSE YOU HAVE RESCUED ME.
I WILL SING TO THE LORD BECAUSE HE HAS BEEN SO GOOD TO ME.
PSALM 13:5-6

_____

_____

_____

_____

_____

_____

_____

_____

_____

_____

_____

_____

_____

_____

_____

_____

_____

_____

_____

_____

_____

_____

_____

LIVE A LIFE OF LOVE, JUST AS CHRIST LOVED US AND GAVE HIMSELF UP FOR US AS A
FRAGRANT OFFERING AND SACRIFICE TO GOD.
EPHESIANS 5:2

_____

_____

_____

_____

_____

_____

_____

_____

_____

_____

_____

_____

_____

_____

_____

_____

_____

_____

_____

_____

_____

_____

_____

_____

_____

"YOU WILL CALL UPON ME AND COME AND PRAY TO ME, AND I WILL LISTEN TO YOU.
YOU WILL SEEK ME AND FIND ME WHEN YOU SEEK ME WITH ALL YOUR HEART."

JEREMIAH 29:12-13

_____

_____

_____

_____

_____

_____

_____

_____

_____

_____

_____

_____

_____

_____

_____

_____

_____

_____

_____

_____

_____

_____

_____

_____

_____

_____

MY SOUL FINDS REST IN GOD ALONE; MY SALVATION COMES FROM HIM.

PSALM 62:1

_____

_____

_____

_____

_____

_____

_____

_____

_____

_____

_____

_____

_____

_____

_____

_____

_____

_____

_____

_____

_____

_____

_____

_____

DELIGHT YOURSELF IN THE LORD, AND HE WILL GIVE YOU THE DESIRES OF YOUR HEART.

PSALM 37:4

_____

_____

_____

_____

_____

_____

_____

_____

_____

_____

_____

_____

_____

_____

_____

_____

_____

_____

_____

_____

_____

_____

_____

_____

_____

THE LORD IS MY LIGHT AND MY SALVATION—WHOM SHALL I FEAR?
THE LORD IS THE STRONGHOLD OF MY LIFE—OF WHOM SHALL I BE AFRAID?

PSALM 27:1

_____

_____

_____

_____

_____

_____

_____

_____

_____

_____

_____

_____

_____

_____

_____

_____

_____

_____

_____

_____

_____

_____

_____

_____

THE LORD HIMSELF GOES BEFORE YOU AND WILL BE WITH YOU;
HE WILL NEVER LEAVE YOU NOR FORSAKE YOU.

DEUTERONOMY 31:8

_____

_____

_____

_____

_____

_____

_____

_____

_____

_____

_____

_____

_____

_____

_____

_____

_____

_____

_____

_____

_____

_____

_____

GOD IS WORKING IN YOU, GIVING YOU THE DESIRE TO OBEY HIM AND THE POWER TO DO WHAT PLEASES HIM.

PHILIPPIANS 2:13

_____

_____

_____

_____

_____

_____

_____

_____

_____

_____

_____

_____

_____

_____

_____

_____

_____

_____

_____

_____

_____

_____

_____

_____

I CAN DO EVERYTHING THROUGH CHRIST, WHO GIVES ME STRENGTH.

PHILIPPIANS 4:13

_____

_____

_____

_____

_____

_____

_____

_____

_____

_____

_____

_____

_____

_____

_____

_____

_____

_____

_____

_____

_____

_____

_____

IF YOU WANT TO KNOW WHAT GOD WANTS YOU TO DO, ASK HIM, AND HE WILL GLADLY TELL YOU.

JAMES 1:5

_____

_____

_____

_____

_____

_____

_____

_____

_____

_____

_____

_____

_____

_____

_____

_____

_____

_____

_____

_____

_____

_____

_____

_____

CREATE IN ME A PURE HEART, O GOD, AND RENEW A STEADFAST SPIRIT WITHIN ME.

PSALM 51:10

IF ANYONE IS IN CHRIST, HE IS A NEW CREATION; THE OLD HAS GONE, THE NEW HAS COME!

2 CORINTHIANS 5:17

_____

_____

_____

_____

_____

_____

_____

_____

_____

_____

_____

_____

_____

_____

_____

_____

_____

_____

_____

_____

_____

_____

_____

CAST YOUR CARES ON THE LORD AND HE WILL SUSTAIN YOU.

PSALM 55:22

_____

_____

_____

_____

_____

_____

_____

_____

_____

_____

_____

_____

_____

_____

_____

_____

_____

_____

_____

_____

_____

_____

THE LORD YOUR GOD IS WITH YOU, HE IS MIGHTY TO SAVE. HE WILL TAKE GREAT
DELIGHT IN YOU, HE WILL QUIET YOU WITH HIS LOVE.
ZEPHANIAH 3:17

THE LORD IS FAITHFUL TO ALL HIS PROMISES AND LOVING TOWARD ALL HE HAS MADE.

PSALM 145:13

_____

_____

_____

_____

_____

_____

_____

_____

_____

_____

_____

_____

_____

_____

_____

_____

_____

_____

_____

_____

_____

_____

_____

_____

_____

IN YOU, O LORD, DO I PUT MY TRUST AND CONFIDENTLY TAKE REFUGE;
LET ME NEVER BE PUT TO SHAME OR CONFUSION!

PSALM 71:1

_____

_____

_____

_____

_____

_____

_____

_____

_____

_____

_____

_____

_____

_____

_____

_____

_____

_____

_____

_____

_____

_____

_____

_____

_____

"BE STRONG AND COURAGEOUS . . . THE LORD YOUR GOD WILL BE WITH YOU WHEREVER YOU GO."

JOSHUA 1:9

_____

_____

_____

_____

_____

_____

_____

_____

_____

_____

_____

_____

_____

_____

_____

_____

_____

_____

_____

_____

_____

_____

**DEPEND ON THE LORD IN WHATEVER YOU DO,
AND YOUR PLANS WILL SUCCEED.**

PROVERBS 16:3

_____

_____

_____

_____

_____

_____

_____

_____

_____

_____

_____

_____

_____

_____

_____

_____

_____

_____

_____

_____

_____

_____

_____

_____

SINCE WE HAVE BEEN JUSTIFIED THROUGH FAITH,
WE HAVE PEACE WITH GOD THROUGH OUR LORD JESUS CHRIST.

ROMANS 5:1

THE LORD IS MY ROCK, MY FORTRESS AND MY DELIVERER;
MY GOD IS MY ROCK, IN WHOM I TAKE REFUGE.

PSALM 18:2

_____

_____

_____

_____

_____

_____

_____

_____

_____

_____

_____

_____

_____

_____

_____

_____

_____

_____

_____

_____

_____

_____

_____

"IF ANYONE WOULD COME AFTER ME, HE MUST DENY HIMSELF
AND TAKE UP HIS CROSS AND FOLLOW ME."

MATTHEW 16:24

THE WORD OF THE LORD IS RIGHT AND TRUE; HE IS FAITHFUL IN ALL HE DOES.

PSALM 33:4

THE LORD IS MY STRENGTH, MY SHIELD FROM EVERY DANGER. I TRUST IN HIM WITH ALL MY HEART.

PSALM 28:7

IN HIM WE HAVE REDEMPTION THROUGH HIS BLOOD, THE FORGIVENESS OF
SINS, IN ACCORDANCE WITH THE RICHES OF GOD'S GRACE.
EPHESIANS 1:7

_____

_____

_____

_____

_____

_____

_____

_____

_____

_____

_____

_____

_____

_____

_____

_____

_____

_____

_____

_____

_____

I TRUST IN YOUR UNFAILING LOVE. I WILL REJOICE BECAUSE YOU HAVE RESCUED ME.
I WILL SING TO THE LORD BECAUSE HE HAS BEEN SO GOOD TO ME.
PSALM 13:5-6

LIVE A LIFE OF LOVE, JUST AS CHRIST LOVED US AND GAVE HIMSELF UP FOR US AS A
FRAGRANT OFFERING AND SACRIFICE TO GOD.
EPHESIANS 5:2

_____

_____

_____

_____

_____

_____

_____

_____

_____

_____

_____

_____

_____

_____

_____

_____

_____

_____

_____

_____

_____

_____

_____

_____

_____

_____

MY SOUL FINDS REST IN GOD ALONE; MY SALVATION COMES FROM HIM.

PSALM 62:1

DELIGHT YOURSELF IN THE LORD, AND HE WILL GIVE YOU THE DESIRES OF YOUR HEART.

PSALM 37:4

_____

_____

_____

_____

_____

_____

_____

_____

_____

_____

_____

_____

_____

_____

_____

_____

_____

_____

_____

_____

_____

_____

_____

_____

THE LORD IS MY LIGHT AND MY SALVATION—WHOM SHALL I FEAR?
THE LORD IS THE STRONGHOLD OF MY LIFE—OF WHOM SHALL I BE AFRAID?

PSALM 27:1

_____

_____

_____

_____

_____

_____

_____

_____

_____

_____

_____

_____

_____

_____

_____

_____

_____

_____

_____

_____

_____

_____

_____

THE LORD HIMSELF GOES BEFORE YOU AND WILL BE WITH YOU;
HE WILL NEVER LEAVE YOU NOR FORSAKE YOU.

DEUTERONOMY 31:8

GOD IS WORKING IN YOU, GIVING YOU THE DESIRE TO OBEY HIM AND THE POWER TO DO WHAT PLEASES HIM.

PHILIPPIANS 2:13

_____

_____

_____

_____

_____

_____

_____

_____

_____

_____

_____

_____

_____

_____

_____

_____

_____

_____

_____

_____

_____

_____

I CAN DO EVERYTHING THROUGH CHRIST, WHO GIVES ME STRENGTH.

PHILIPPIANS 4:13

_____

_____

_____

_____

_____

_____

_____

_____

_____

_____

_____

_____

_____

_____

_____

_____

_____

_____

_____

_____

_____

_____

_____

_____

_____

_____

IF YOU WANT TO KNOW WHAT GOD WANTS YOU TO DO, ASK HIM, AND HE WILL GLADLY TELL YOU.

JAMES 1:5

CREATE IN ME A PURE HEART, O GOD, AND RENEW A STEADFAST SPIRIT WITHIN ME.

PSALM 51:10

IF ANYONE IS IN CHRIST, HE IS A NEW CREATION; THE OLD HAS GONE, THE NEW HAS COME!

2 CORINTHIANS 5:17

_____

_____

_____

_____

_____

_____

_____

_____

_____

_____

_____

_____

_____

_____

_____

_____

_____

_____

_____

_____

_____

_____

_____

_____

_____

_____

CAST YOUR CARES ON THE LORD AND HE WILL SUSTAIN YOU.

PSALM 55:22

_____

_____

_____

_____

_____

_____

_____

_____

_____

_____

_____

_____

_____

_____

_____

_____

_____

_____

_____

_____

_____

_____

_____

THE LORD YOUR GOD IS WITH YOU, HE IS MIGHTY TO SAVE. HE WILL TAKE GREAT
DELIGHT IN YOU, HE WILL QUIET YOU WITH HIS LOVE.
ZEPHANIAH 3:17

_____

_____

_____

_____

_____

_____

_____

_____

_____

_____

_____

_____

_____

_____

_____

_____

_____

_____

_____

_____

_____

_____

_____

THE LORD IS FAITHFUL TO ALL HIS PROMISES AND LOVING TOWARD ALL HE HAS MADE.

PSALM 145:13

_____

_____

_____

_____

_____

_____

_____

_____

_____

_____

_____

_____

_____

_____

_____

_____

_____

_____

_____

_____

_____

_____

_____

**IN YOU, O LORD, DO I PUT MY TRUST AND CONFIDENTLY TAKE REFUGE;
LET ME NEVER BE PUT TO SHAME OR CONFUSION!**

PSALM 71:1

_____

_____

_____

_____

_____

_____

_____

_____

_____

_____

_____

_____

_____

_____

_____

_____

_____

_____

_____

_____

_____

_____

_____

_____

_____

_____

"BE STRONG AND COURAGEOUS . . . THE LORD YOUR GOD WILL BE WITH YOU WHEREVER YOU GO."

JOSHUA 1:9

DEPEND ON THE LORD IN WHATEVER YOU DO,
AND YOUR PLANS WILL SUCCEED.

PROVERBS 16:3

_____

_____

_____

_____

_____

_____

_____

_____

_____

_____

_____

_____

_____

_____

_____

_____

_____

_____

_____

_____

_____

_____

SINCE WE HAVE BEEN JUSTIFIED THROUGH FAITH,
WE HAVE PEACE WITH GOD THROUGH OUR LORD JESUS CHRIST.

ROMANS 5:1

_____

_____

_____

_____

_____

_____

_____

_____

_____

_____

_____

_____

_____

_____

_____

_____

_____

_____

_____

_____

_____

_____

_____

_____

THE LORD IS MY ROCK, MY FORTRESS AND MY DELIVERER;
MY GOD IS MY ROCK, IN WHOM I TAKE REFUGE.

PSALM 18:2

_____

_____

_____

_____

_____

_____

_____

_____

_____

_____

_____

_____

_____

_____

_____

_____

_____

_____

_____

_____

_____

_____

_____

_____

**"IF ANYONE WOULD COME AFTER ME, HE MUST DENY HIMSELF
AND TAKE UP HIS CROSS AND FOLLOW ME."**

MATTHEW 16:24

_____
_____
_____
_____
_____
_____
_____
_____
_____
_____
_____
_____
_____
_____
_____
_____
_____
_____
_____
_____
_____
_____
_____
_____
_____

THE WORD OF THE LORD IS RIGHT AND TRUE; HE IS FAITHFUL IN ALL HE DOES.

PSALM 33:4

_____

_____

_____

_____

_____

_____

_____

_____

_____

_____

_____

_____

_____

_____

_____

_____

_____

_____

_____

_____

_____

_____

_____

_____

_____

THE LORD IS MY STRENGTH, MY SHIELD FROM EVERY DANGER. I TRUST IN HIM WITH ALL MY HEART.

PSALM 28:7

IN HIM WE HAVE REDEMPTION THROUGH HIS BLOOD, THE FORGIVENESS OF
SINS, IN ACCORDANCE WITH THE RICHES OF GOD'S GRACE.
EPHESIANS 1:7

_____

_____

_____

_____

_____

_____

_____

_____

_____

_____

_____

_____

_____

_____

_____

_____

_____

_____

_____

_____

_____

_____

I TRUST IN YOUR UNFAILING LOVE. I WILL REJOICE BECAUSE YOU HAVE RESCUED ME.
I WILL SING TO THE LORD BECAUSE HE HAS BEEN SO GOOD TO ME.
PSALM 13:5-6

_____

_____

_____

_____

_____

_____

_____

_____

_____

_____

_____

_____

_____

_____

_____

_____

_____

_____

_____

_____

_____

_____

_____

_____

LIVE A LIFE OF LOVE, JUST AS CHRIST LOVED US AND GAVE HIMSELF UP FOR US AS A
FRAGRANT OFFERING AND SACRIFICE TO GOD.
EPHESIANS 5:2

_____

_____

_____

_____

_____

_____

_____

_____

_____

_____

_____

_____

_____

_____

_____

_____

_____

_____

_____

_____

_____

_____

_____

_____

_____

"YOU WILL CALL UPON ME AND COME AND PRAY TO ME, AND I WILL LISTEN TO YOU.
YOU WILL SEEK ME AND FIND ME WHEN YOU SEEK ME WITH ALL YOUR HEART."

JEREMIAH 29:12-13

_____

_____

_____

_____

_____

_____

_____

_____

_____

_____

_____

_____

_____

_____

_____

_____

_____

_____

_____

_____

_____

_____

_____

_____

_____

_____

_____

MY SOUL FINDS REST IN GOD ALONE; MY SALVATION COMES FROM HIM.

PSALM 62:1

_____

_____

_____

_____

_____

_____

_____

_____

_____

_____

_____

_____

_____

_____

_____

_____

_____

_____

_____

_____

_____

_____

_____

_____

_____

THE LORD IS MY LIGHT AND MY SALVATION—WHOM SHALL I FEAR?
THE LORD IS THE STRONGHOLD OF MY LIFE—OF WHOM SHALL I BE AFRAID?

PSALM 27:1

_____

_____

_____

_____

_____

_____

_____

_____

_____

_____

_____

_____

_____

_____

_____

_____

_____

_____

_____

_____

_____

_____

_____

THE LORD HIMSELF GOES BEFORE YOU AND WILL BE WITH YOU;
HE WILL NEVER LEAVE YOU NOR FORSAKE YOU.

DEUTERONOMY 31:8

_____

_____

_____

_____

_____

_____

_____

_____

_____

_____

_____

_____

_____

_____

_____

_____

_____

_____

_____

_____

_____

_____

_____

_____

_____

_____

GOD IS WORKING IN YOU, GIVING YOU THE DESIRE TO OBEY HIM AND THE POWER TO DO WHAT PLEASES HIM.

PHILIPPIANS 2:13

_____

_____

_____

_____

_____

_____

_____

_____

_____

_____

_____

_____

_____

_____

_____

_____

_____

_____

_____

_____

_____

_____

_____

I CAN DO EVERYTHING THROUGH CHRIST, WHO GIVES ME STRENGTH.

PHILIPPIANS 4:13

_____

_____

_____

_____

_____

_____

_____

_____

_____

_____

_____

_____

_____

_____

_____

_____

_____

_____

_____

_____

_____

_____

_____

_____

IF YOU WANT TO KNOW WHAT GOD WANTS YOU TO DO, ASK HIM, AND HE WILL GLADLY TELL YOU.

JAMES 1:5

_____

_____

_____

_____

_____

_____

_____

_____

_____

_____

_____

_____

_____

_____

_____

_____

_____

_____

_____

_____

_____

_____

CREATE IN ME A PURE HEART, O GOD, AND RENEW A STEADFAST SPIRIT WITHIN ME.

PSALM 51:10

_____

_____

_____

_____

_____

_____

_____

_____

_____

_____

_____

_____

_____

_____

_____

_____

_____

_____

_____

_____

_____

_____

_____

_____

CAST YOUR CARES ON THE LORD AND HE WILL SUSTAIN YOU.

PSALM 55:22

_____

_____

_____

_____

_____

_____

_____

_____

_____

_____

_____

_____

_____

_____

_____

_____

_____

_____

_____

_____

_____

_____

_____

_____

_____

**THE LORD YOUR GOD IS WITH YOU, HE IS MIGHTY TO SAVE. HE WILL TAKE GREAT
DELIGHT IN YOU, HE WILL QUIET YOU WITH HIS LOVE.**
ZEPHANIAH 3:17

_____

_____

_____

_____

_____

_____

_____

_____

_____

_____

_____

_____

_____

_____

_____

_____

_____

_____

_____

_____

_____

_____

_____

_____

THE LORD IS FAITHFUL TO ALL HIS PROMISES AND LOVING TOWARD ALL HE HAS MADE.

PSALM 145:13

_____

_____

_____

_____

_____

_____

_____

_____

_____

_____

_____

_____

_____

_____

_____

_____

_____

_____

_____

_____

_____

_____

_____

_____

_____

_____

_____

IN YOU, O LORD, DO I PUT MY TRUST AND CONFIDENTLY TAKE REFUGE;
LET ME NEVER BE PUT TO SHAME OR CONFUSION!

PSALM 71:1

DEPEND ON THE LORD IN WHATEVER YOU DO,
AND YOUR PLANS WILL SUCCEED.

PROVERBS 16:3

SINCE WE HAVE BEEN JUSTIFIED THROUGH FAITH,
WE HAVE PEACE WITH GOD THROUGH OUR LORD JESUS CHRIST.

ROMANS 5:1

_____

_____

_____

_____

_____

_____

_____

_____

_____

_____

_____

_____

_____

_____

_____

_____

_____

_____

_____

_____

_____

_____

_____

_____

**THE LORD IS MY ROCK, MY FORTRESS AND MY DELIVERER;
MY GOD IS MY ROCK, IN WHOM I TAKE REFUGE.**

PSALM 18:2

_____

_____

_____

_____

_____

_____

_____

_____

_____

_____

_____

_____

_____

_____

_____

_____

_____

_____

_____

_____

_____

_____

_____

_____

_____

_____

_____

**"IF ANYONE WOULD COME AFTER ME, HE MUST DENY HIMSELF
AND TAKE UP HIS CROSS AND FOLLOW ME."**

MATTHEW 16:24

_____

_____

_____

_____

_____

_____

_____

_____

_____

_____

_____

_____

_____

_____

_____

_____

_____

_____

_____

_____

_____

_____

_____

THE WORD OF THE LORD IS RIGHT AND TRUE; HE IS FAITHFUL IN ALL HE DOES.

PSALM 33:4

THE LORD IS MY STRENGTH, MY SHIELD FROM EVERY DANGER. I TRUST IN HIM WITH ALL MY HEART.

PSALM 28:7

_____

_____

_____

_____

_____

_____

_____

_____

_____

_____

_____

_____

_____

_____

_____

_____

_____

_____

_____

_____

_____

_____

_____

_____

_____

LIVE A LIFE OF LOVE, JUST AS CHRIST LOVED US AND GAVE HIMSELF UP FOR US AS A
FRAGRANT OFFERING AND SACRIFICE TO GOD.

EPHESIANS 5:2

_____

_____

_____

_____

_____

_____

_____

_____

_____

_____

_____

_____

_____

_____

_____

_____

_____

_____

_____

_____

_____

_____

_____

_____

_____

_____

_____

"YOU WILL CALL UPON ME AND COME AND PRAY TO ME, AND I WILL LISTEN TO YOU.
YOU WILL SEEK ME AND FIND ME WHEN YOU SEEK ME WITH ALL YOUR HEART."

JEREMIAH 29:12-13

_____

_____

_____

_____

_____

_____

_____

_____

_____

_____

_____

_____

_____

_____

_____

_____

_____

_____

_____

_____

_____

_____

_____

MY SOUL FINDS REST IN GOD ALONE; MY SALVATION COMES FROM HIM.

PSALM 62:1

DELIGHT YOURSELF IN THE LORD, AND HE WILL GIVE YOU THE DESIRES OF YOUR HEART.

PSALM 37:4

_____

_____

_____

_____

_____

_____

_____

_____

_____

_____

_____

_____

_____

_____

_____

_____

_____

_____

_____

_____

_____

_____

_____

THE LORD HIMSELF GOES BEFORE YOU AND WILL BE WITH YOU;
HE WILL NEVER LEAVE YOU NOR FORSAKE YOU.

DEUTERONOMY 31:8

_____

_____

_____

_____

_____

_____

_____

_____

_____

_____

_____

_____

_____

_____

_____

_____

_____

_____

_____

_____

_____

_____

_____

GOD IS WORKING IN YOU, GIVING YOU THE DESIRE TO OBEY HIM AND THE POWER TO DO WHAT PLEASES HIM.

PHILIPPIANS 2:13

I CAN DO EVERYTHING THROUGH CHRIST, WHO GIVES ME STRENGTH.

PHILIPPIANS 4:13

_____

_____

_____

_____

_____

_____

_____

_____

_____

_____

_____

_____

_____

_____

_____

_____

_____

_____

_____

_____

_____

_____

_____

IF YOU WANT TO KNOW WHAT GOD WANTS YOU TO DO, ASK HIM, AND HE WILL GLADLY TELL YOU.

JAMES 1:5

CREATE IN ME A PURE HEART, O GOD, AND RENEW A STEADFAST SPIRIT WITHIN ME.

PSALM 51:10

IF ANYONE IS IN CHRIST, HE IS A NEW CREATION; THE OLD HAS GONE, THE NEW HAS COME!

2 CORINTHIANS 5:17

_____

_____

_____

_____

_____

_____

_____

_____

_____

_____

_____

_____

_____

_____

_____

_____

_____

_____

_____

_____

_____

_____

_____

_____

CAST YOUR CARES ON THE LORD AND HE WILL SUSTAIN YOU.

PSALM 55:22

_____

_____

_____

_____

_____

_____

_____

_____

_____

_____

_____

_____

_____

_____

_____

_____

_____

_____

_____

_____

_____

_____

_____

_____

_____

THE LORD YOUR GOD IS WITH YOU, HE IS MIGHTY TO SAVE. HE WILL TAKE GREAT
DELIGHT IN YOU, HE WILL QUIET YOU WITH HIS LOVE.
ZEPHANIAH 3:17

THE LORD IS FAITHFUL TO ALL HIS PROMISES AND LOVING TOWARD ALL HE HAS MADE.

PSALM 145:13

_____

_____

_____

_____

_____

_____

_____

_____

_____

_____

_____

_____

_____

_____

_____

_____

_____

_____

_____

_____

_____

_____

_____

_____

_____

_____

**IN YOU, O LORD, DO I PUT MY TRUST AND CONFIDENTLY TAKE REFUGE;
LET ME NEVER BE PUT TO SHAME OR CONFUSION!**

PSALM 71:1

_____

_____

_____

_____

_____

_____

_____

_____

_____

_____

_____

_____

_____

_____

_____

_____

_____

_____

_____

_____

_____

_____

_____

_____

_____

"BE STRONG AND COURAGEOUS . . . THE LORD YOUR GOD WILL BE WITH YOU WHEREVER YOU GO."

JOSHUA 1:9

_____

_____

_____

_____

_____

_____

_____

_____

_____

_____

_____

_____

_____

_____

_____

_____

_____

_____

_____

_____

_____

_____

_____

**SINCE WE HAVE BEEN JUSTIFIED THROUGH FAITH,
WE HAVE PEACE WITH GOD THROUGH OUR LORD JESUS CHRIST.**

ROMANS 5:1

THE LORD IS MY ROCK, MY FORTRESS AND MY DELIVERER;
MY GOD IS MY ROCK, IN WHOM I TAKE REFUGE.

PSALM 18:2

_____

_____

_____

_____

_____

_____

_____

_____

_____

_____

_____

_____

_____

_____

_____

_____

_____

_____

_____

_____

_____

_____

_____

"IF ANYONE WOULD COME AFTER ME, HE MUST DENY HIMSELF
AND TAKE UP HIS CROSS AND FOLLOW ME."

MATTHEW 16:24

THE WORD OF THE LORD IS RIGHT AND TRUE; HE IS FAITHFUL IN ALL HE DOES.

PSALM 33:4

_____

_____

_____

_____

_____

_____

_____

_____

_____

_____

_____

_____

_____

_____

_____

_____

_____

_____

_____

_____

_____

_____

_____

_____

THE LORD IS MY STRENGTH, MY SHIELD FROM EVERY DANGER. I TRUST IN HIM WITH ALL MY HEART.

PSALM 28:7

_____

_____

_____

_____

_____

_____

_____

_____

_____

_____

_____

_____

_____

_____

_____

_____

_____

_____

_____

_____

_____

_____

_____

_____

IN HIM WE HAVE REDEMPTION THROUGH HIS BLOOD, THE FORGIVENESS OF
SINS, IN ACCORDANCE WITH THE RICHES OF GOD'S GRACE.

EPHESIANS 1:7

_____

_____

_____

_____

_____

_____

_____

_____

_____

_____

_____

_____

_____

_____

_____

_____

_____

_____

_____

_____

_____

_____

_____

_____

_____

I TRUST IN YOUR UNFAILING LOVE. I WILL REJOICE BECAUSE YOU HAVE RESCUED ME.
I WILL SING TO THE LORD BECAUSE HE HAS BEEN SO GOOD TO ME.
PSALM 13:5-6

LIVE A LIFE OF LOVE, JUST AS CHRIST LOVED US AND GAVE HIMSELF UP FOR US AS A
FRAGRANT OFFERING AND SACRIFICE TO GOD.
EPHESIANS 5:2

_____

_____

_____

_____

_____

_____

_____

_____

_____

_____

_____

_____

_____

_____

_____

_____

_____

_____

_____

_____

_____

_____

_____

_____

_____

_____

_____

_____

"YOU WILL CALL UPON ME AND COME AND PRAY TO ME, AND I WILL LISTEN TO YOU.
YOU WILL SEEK ME AND FIND ME WHEN YOU SEEK ME WITH ALL YOUR HEART."

JEREMIAH 29:12-13

MY SOUL FINDS REST IN GOD ALONE; MY SALVATION COMES FROM HIM.

PSALM 62:1

_____

_____

_____

_____

_____

_____

_____

_____

_____

_____

_____

_____

_____

_____

_____

_____

_____

_____

_____

_____

_____

_____

DELIGHT YOURSELF IN THE LORD, AND HE WILL GIVE YOU THE DESIRES OF YOUR HEART.

PSALM 37:4

_____

_____

_____

_____

_____

_____

_____

_____

_____

_____

_____

_____

_____

_____

_____

_____

_____

_____

_____

_____

_____

_____

_____

_____

THE LORD IS MY LIGHT AND MY SALVATION—WHOM SHALL I FEAR?
THE LORD IS THE STRONGHOLD OF MY LIFE—OF WHOM SHALL I BE AFRAID?

PSALM 27:1

**THE LORD HIMSELF GOES BEFORE YOU AND WILL BE WITH YOU;
HE WILL NEVER LEAVE YOU NOR FORSAKE YOU.**

DEUTERONOMY 31:8

_____

_____

_____

_____

_____

_____

_____

_____

_____

_____

_____

_____

_____

_____

_____

_____

_____

_____

_____

_____

_____

_____

_____

GOD IS WORKING IN YOU, GIVING YOU THE DESIRE TO OBEY HIM AND THE POWER TO DO WHAT PLEASES HIM.

PHILIPPIANS 2:13

_____

_____

_____

_____

_____

_____

_____

_____

_____

_____

_____

_____

_____

_____

_____

_____

_____

_____

_____

_____

_____

_____

_____

I CAN DO EVERYTHING THROUGH CHRIST, WHO GIVES ME STRENGTH.

PHILIPPIANS 4:13

_____

_____

_____

_____

_____

_____

_____

_____

_____

_____

_____

_____

_____

_____

_____

_____

_____

_____

_____

_____

_____

_____

IF YOU WANT TO KNOW WHAT GOD WANTS YOU TO DO, ASK HIM, AND HE WILL GLADLY TELL YOU.

JAMES 1:5

CREATE IN ME A PURE HEART, O GOD, AND RENEW A STEADFAST SPIRIT WITHIN ME.

PSALM 51:10

IF ANYONE IS IN CHRIST, HE IS A NEW CREATION; THE OLD HAS GONE, THE NEW HAS COME!

2 CORINTHIANS 5:17

_____

_____

_____

_____

_____

_____

_____

_____

_____

_____

_____

_____

_____

_____

_____

_____

_____

_____

_____

_____

_____

_____

CAST YOUR CARES ON THE LORD AND HE WILL SUSTAIN YOU.

PSALM 55:22

_____

_____

_____

_____

_____

_____

_____

_____

_____

_____

_____

_____

_____

_____

_____

_____

_____

_____

_____

_____

_____

_____

_____

_____

THE LORD YOUR GOD IS WITH YOU, HE IS MIGHTY TO SAVE. HE WILL TAKE GREAT
DELIGHT IN YOU, HE WILL QUIET YOU WITH HIS LOVE.

ZEPHANIAH 3:17

THE LORD IS FAITHFUL TO ALL HIS PROMISES AND LOVING TOWARD ALL HE HAS MADE.

PSALM 145:13

_____

_____

_____

_____

_____

_____

_____

_____

_____

_____

_____

_____

_____

_____

_____

_____

_____

_____

_____

_____

_____

_____

_____

_____

_____

_____

_____

_____

IN YOU, O LORD, DO I PUT MY TRUST AND CONFIDENTLY TAKE REFUGE;
LET ME NEVER BE PUT TO SHAME OR CONFUSION!

PSALM 71:1

_____

_____

_____

_____

_____

_____

_____

_____

_____

_____

_____

_____

_____

_____

_____

_____

_____

_____

_____

_____

_____

_____

_____

_____

"BE STRONG AND COURAGEOUS . . . THE LORD YOUR GOD WILL BE WITH YOU WHEREVER YOU GO."

JOSHUA 1:9

_____

_____

_____

_____

_____

_____

_____

_____

_____

_____

_____

_____

_____

_____

_____

_____

_____

_____

_____

_____

_____

_____

_____

_____

**DEPEND ON THE LORD IN WHATEVER YOU DO,
AND YOUR PLANS WILL SUCCEED.**

PROVERBS 16:3

_____

_____

_____

_____

_____

_____

_____

_____

_____

_____

_____

_____

_____

_____

_____

_____

_____

_____

_____

_____

_____

_____

_____

_____

_____

**SINCE WE HAVE BEEN JUSTIFIED THROUGH FAITH,
WE HAVE PEACE WITH GOD THROUGH OUR LORD JESUS CHRIST.**

ROMANS 5:1

_____

_____

_____

_____

_____

_____

_____

_____

_____

_____

_____

_____

_____

_____

_____

_____

_____

_____

_____

_____

_____

_____

_____

_____

_____

_____

"IF ANYONE WOULD COME AFTER ME, HE MUST DENY HIMSELF
AND TAKE UP HIS CROSS AND FOLLOW ME."

MATTHEW 16:24

_____

_____

_____

_____

_____

_____

_____

_____

_____

_____

_____

_____

_____

_____

_____

_____

_____

_____

_____

_____

_____

_____

_____

_____

_____

THE WORD OF THE LORD IS RIGHT AND TRUE; HE IS FAITHFUL IN ALL HE DOES.

PSALM 33:4

THE LORD IS MY STRENGTH, MY SHIELD FROM EVERY DANGER. I TRUST IN HIM WITH ALL MY HEART.

PSALM 28:7

LIVE A LIFE OF LOVE, JUST AS CHRIST LOVED US AND GAVE HIMSELF UP FOR US AS A
FRAGRANT OFFERING AND SACRIFICE TO GOD.

EPHESIANS 5:2

_____

_____

_____

_____

_____

_____

_____

_____

_____

_____

_____

_____

_____

_____

_____

_____

_____

_____

_____

_____

_____

_____

_____

"YOU WILL CALL UPON ME AND COME AND PRAY TO ME, AND I WILL LISTEN TO YOU.
YOU WILL SEEK ME AND FIND ME WHEN YOU SEEK ME WITH ALL YOUR HEART."

JEREMIAH 29:12-13

_____

_____

_____

_____

_____

_____

_____

_____

_____

_____

_____

_____

_____

_____

_____

_____

_____

_____

_____

_____

_____

_____

MY SOUL FINDS REST IN GOD ALONE; MY SALVATION COMES FROM HIM.

PSALM 62:1

_____

_____

_____

_____

_____

_____

_____

_____

_____

_____

_____

_____

_____

_____

_____

_____

_____

_____

_____

_____

_____

_____

_____

_____

_____

DELIGHT YOURSELF IN THE LORD, AND HE WILL GIVE YOU THE DESIRES OF YOUR HEART.

PSALM 37:4

_____

_____

_____

_____

_____

_____

_____

_____

_____

_____

_____

_____

_____

_____

_____

_____

_____

_____

_____

_____

_____

_____

_____

_____

_____

THE LORD IS MY LIGHT AND MY SALVATION—WHOM SHALL I FEAR?
THE LORD IS THE STRONGHOLD OF MY LIFE—OF WHOM SHALL I BE AFRAID?

PSALM 27:1

THE LORD HIMSELF GOES BEFORE YOU AND WILL BE WITH YOU;
HE WILL NEVER LEAVE YOU NOR FORSAKE YOU.

DEUTERONOMY 31:8

GOD IS WORKING IN YOU, GIVING YOU THE DESIRE TO OBEY HIM AND THE POWER TO DO WHAT PLEASES HIM.

PHILIPPIANS 2:13

I CAN DO EVERYTHING THROUGH CHRIST, WHO GIVES ME STRENGTH.

PHILIPPIANS 4:13

_____

_____

_____

_____

_____

_____

_____

_____

_____

_____

_____

_____

_____

_____

_____

_____

_____

_____

_____

_____

_____

_____

_____

IF YOU WANT TO KNOW WHAT GOD WANTS YOU TO DO, ASK HIM, AND HE WILL GLADLY TELL YOU.

JAMES 1:5

_____

_____

_____

_____

_____

_____

_____

_____

_____

_____

_____

_____

_____

_____

_____

_____

_____

_____

_____

_____

_____

_____

_____

_____

_____

CREATE IN ME A PURE HEART, O GOD, AND RENEW A STEADFAST SPIRIT WITHIN ME.

PSALM 51:10

IF ANYONE IS IN CHRIST, HE IS A NEW CREATION; THE OLD HAS GONE, THE NEW HAS COME!

2 CORINTHIANS 5:17

_____

_____

_____

_____

_____

_____

_____

_____

_____

_____

_____

_____

_____

_____

_____

_____

_____

_____

_____

_____

_____

_____

_____

_____

_____

CAST YOUR CARES ON THE LORD AND HE WILL SUSTAIN YOU.

PSALM 55:22

THE LORD YOUR GOD IS WITH YOU, HE IS MIGHTY TO SAVE. HE WILL TAKE GREAT
DELIGHT IN YOU, HE WILL QUIET YOU WITH HIS LOVE.

ZEPHANIAH 3:17

_____

_____

_____

_____

_____

_____

_____

_____

_____

_____

_____

_____

_____

_____

_____

_____

_____

_____

_____

_____

_____

_____

_____

THE LORD IS FAITHFUL TO ALL HIS PROMISES AND LOVING TOWARD ALL HE HAS MADE.

PSALM 145:13

IN YOU, O LORD, DO I PUT MY TRUST AND CONFIDENTLY TAKE REFUGE;
LET ME NEVER BE PUT TO SHAME OR CONFUSION!

PSALM 71:1

_____

_____

_____

_____

_____

_____

_____

_____

_____

_____

_____

_____

_____

_____

_____

_____

_____

_____

_____

_____

_____

_____

_____

_____

"BE STRONG AND COURAGEOUS . . . THE LORD YOUR GOD WILL BE WITH YOU WHEREVER YOU GO."

JOSHUA 1:9

_____

_____

_____

_____

_____

_____

_____

_____

_____

_____

_____

_____

_____

_____

_____

_____

_____

_____

_____

_____

_____

_____

_____

_____

DEPEND ON THE LORD IN WHATEVER YOU DO,
AND YOUR PLANS WILL SUCCEED.

PROVERBS 16:3

_____

_____

_____

_____

_____

_____

_____

_____

_____

_____

_____

_____

_____

_____

_____

_____

_____

_____

_____

_____

_____

_____

_____

_____

_____

**SINCE WE HAVE BEEN JUSTIFIED THROUGH FAITH,
WE HAVE PEACE WITH GOD THROUGH OUR LORD JESUS CHRIST.**

ROMANS 5:1

_____

_____

_____

_____

_____

_____

_____

_____

_____

_____

_____

_____

_____

_____

_____

_____

_____

_____

_____

_____

_____

_____

_____

_____

THE LORD IS MY ROCK, MY FORTRESS AND MY DELIVERER;
MY GOD IS MY ROCK, IN WHOM I TAKE REFUGE.

PSALM 18:2

"IF ANYONE WOULD COME AFTER ME, HE MUST DENY HIMSELF
AND TAKE UP HIS CROSS AND FOLLOW ME."

MATTHEW 16:24

THE WORD OF THE LORD IS RIGHT AND TRUE; HE IS FAITHFUL IN ALL HE DOES.

PSALM 33:4

_____

_____

_____

_____

_____

_____

_____

_____

_____

_____

_____

_____

_____

_____

_____

_____

_____

_____

_____

_____

_____

_____

_____

_____

_____

THE LORD IS MY STRENGTH, MY SHIELD FROM EVERY DANGER. I TRUST IN HIM WITH ALL MY HEART.

PSALM 28:7

_____

_____

_____

_____

_____

_____

_____

_____

_____

_____

_____

_____

_____

_____

_____

_____

_____

_____

_____

_____

_____

_____

_____

_____

**IN HIM WE HAVE REDEMPTION THROUGH HIS BLOOD, THE FORGIVENESS OF
SINS, IN ACCORDANCE WITH THE RICHES OF GOD'S GRACE.**
EPHESIANS 1:7

_____

_____

_____

_____

_____

_____

_____

_____

_____

_____

_____

_____

_____

_____

_____

_____

_____

_____

_____

_____

_____

_____

_____

I TRUST IN YOUR UNFAILING LOVE. I WILL REJOICE BECAUSE YOU HAVE RESCUED ME.
I WILL SING TO THE LORD BECAUSE HE HAS BEEN SO GOOD TO ME.
PSALM 13:5-6

_____

_____

_____

_____

_____

_____

_____

_____

_____

_____

_____

_____

_____

_____

_____

_____

_____

_____

_____

_____

_____

_____

_____

_____

_____

LIVE A LIFE OF LOVE, JUST AS CHRIST LOVED US AND GAVE HIMSELF UP FOR US AS A
FRAGRANT OFFERING AND SACRIFICE TO GOD.
EPHESIANS 5:2

_____

_____

_____

_____

_____

_____

_____

_____

_____

_____

_____

_____

_____

_____

_____

_____

_____

_____

_____

_____

_____

_____

_____

"YOU WILL CALL UPON ME AND COME AND PRAY TO ME, AND I WILL LISTEN TO YOU.
YOU WILL SEEK ME AND FIND ME WHEN YOU SEEK ME WITH ALL YOUR HEART."

JEREMIAH 29:12-13

_____

_____

_____

_____

_____

_____

_____

_____

_____

_____

_____

_____

_____

_____

_____

_____

_____

_____

_____

_____

_____

_____

_____

_____

MY SOUL FINDS REST IN GOD ALONE; MY SALVATION COMES FROM HIM.

PSALM 62:1

DELIGHT YOURSELF IN THE LORD, AND HE WILL GIVE YOU THE DESIRES OF YOUR HEART.

PSALM 37:4

_____

_____

_____

_____

_____

_____

_____

_____

_____

_____

_____

_____

_____

_____

_____

_____

_____

_____

_____

_____

_____

_____

_____

THE LORD IS MY LIGHT AND MY SALVATION—WHOM SHALL I FEAR?
THE LORD IS THE STRONGHOLD OF MY LIFE—OF WHOM SHALL I BE AFRAID?

PSALM 27:1

_____

_____

_____

_____

_____

_____

_____

_____

_____

_____

_____

_____

_____

_____

_____

_____

_____

_____

_____

_____

_____

_____

_____

_____

THE LORD HIMSELF GOES BEFORE YOU AND WILL BE WITH YOU;
HE WILL NEVER LEAVE YOU NOR FORSAKE YOU.

DEUTERONOMY 31:8

_____
_____
_____
_____
_____
_____
_____
_____
_____
_____
_____
_____
_____
_____
_____
_____
_____
_____
_____
_____
_____
_____
_____
_____
_____

GOD IS WORKING IN YOU, GIVING YOU THE DESIRE TO OBEY HIM AND THE POWER TO DO WHAT PLEASES HIM.

PHILIPPIANS 2:13

_____

_____

_____

_____

_____

_____

_____

_____

_____

_____

_____

_____

_____

_____

_____

_____

_____

_____

_____

_____

_____

_____

_____

I CAN DO EVERYTHING THROUGH CHRIST, WHO GIVES ME STRENGTH.

PHILIPPIANS 4:13

_____

_____

_____

_____

_____

_____

_____

_____

_____

_____

_____

_____

_____

_____

_____

_____

_____

_____

_____

_____

_____

_____

_____

_____

_____

IF YOU WANT TO KNOW WHAT GOD WANTS YOU TO DO, ASK HIM, AND HE WILL GLADLY TELL YOU.

JAMES 1:5

_____

_____

_____

_____

_____

_____

_____

_____

_____

_____

_____

_____

_____

_____

_____

_____

_____

_____

_____

_____

_____

_____

_____

_____

_____

CREATE IN ME A PURE HEART, O GOD, AND RENEW A STEADFAST SPIRIT WITHIN ME.

PSALM 51:10

IF ANYONE IS IN CHRIST, HE IS A NEW CREATION; THE OLD HAS GONE, THE NEW HAS COME!

2 CORINTHIANS 5:17

CAST YOUR CARES ON THE LORD AND HE WILL SUSTAIN YOU.

PSALM 55:22

THE LORD YOUR GOD IS WITH YOU, HE IS MIGHTY TO SAVE. HE WILL TAKE GREAT
DELIGHT IN YOU, HE WILL QUIET YOU WITH HIS LOVE.
ZEPHANIAH 3:17

THE LORD IS FAITHFUL TO ALL HIS PROMISES AND LOVING TOWARD ALL HE HAS MADE.

PSALM 145:13

**IN YOU, O LORD, DO I PUT MY TRUST AND CONFIDENTLY TAKE REFUGE;
LET ME NEVER BE PUT TO SHAME OR CONFUSION!**

PSALM 71:1

_____

_____

_____

_____

_____

_____

_____

_____

_____

_____

_____

_____

_____

_____

_____

_____

_____

_____

_____

_____

_____

_____

_____

"BE STRONG AND COURAGEOUS . . . THE LORD YOUR GOD WILL BE WITH YOU WHEREVER YOU GO."

JOSHUA 1:9

SINCE WE HAVE BEEN JUSTIFIED THROUGH FAITH,
WE HAVE PEACE WITH GOD THROUGH OUR LORD JESUS CHRIST.

ROMANS 5:1

THE LORD IS MY ROCK, MY FORTRESS AND MY DELIVERER;
MY GOD IS MY ROCK, IN WHOM I TAKE REFUGE.

PSALM 18:2

"IF ANYONE WOULD COME AFTER ME, HE MUST DENY HIMSELF
AND TAKE UP HIS CROSS AND FOLLOW ME."

MATTHEW 16:24

THE WORD OF THE LORD IS RIGHT AND TRUE; HE IS FAITHFUL IN ALL HE DOES.

PSALM 33:4

_____

_____

_____

_____

_____

_____

_____

_____

_____

_____

_____

_____

_____

_____

_____

_____

_____

_____

_____

_____

_____

_____

_____

_____

THE LORD IS MY STRENGTH, MY SHIELD FROM EVERY DANGER. I TRUST IN HIM WITH ALL MY HEART.

PSALM 28:7

_____

_____

_____

_____

_____

_____

_____

_____

_____

_____

_____

_____

_____

_____

_____

_____

_____

_____

_____

_____

_____

_____

_____

_____

**IN HIM WE HAVE REDEMPTION THROUGH HIS BLOOD, THE FORGIVENESS OF
SINS, IN ACCORDANCE WITH THE RICHES OF GOD'S GRACE.**
EPHESIANS 1:7

_____

_____

_____

_____

_____

_____

_____

_____

_____

_____

_____

_____

_____

_____

_____

_____

_____

_____

_____

_____

_____

_____

_____

_____

I TRUST IN YOUR UNFAILING LOVE. I WILL REJOICE BECAUSE YOU HAVE RESCUED ME.
I WILL SING TO THE LORD BECAUSE HE HAS BEEN SO GOOD TO ME.
PSALM 13:5-6

_____

_____

_____

_____

_____

_____

_____

_____

_____

_____

_____

_____

_____

_____

_____

_____

_____

_____

_____

_____

_____

_____

_____

LIVE A LIFE OF LOVE, JUST AS CHRIST LOVED US AND GAVE HIMSELF UP FOR US AS A
FRAGRANT OFFERING AND SACRIFICE TO GOD.
EPHESIANS 5:2

"YOU WILL CALL UPON ME AND COME AND PRAY TO ME, AND I WILL LISTEN TO YOU.
YOU WILL SEEK ME AND FIND ME WHEN YOU SEEK ME WITH ALL YOUR HEART."

JEREMIAH 29:12-13

_____

_____

_____

_____

_____

_____

_____

_____

_____

_____

_____

_____

_____

_____

_____

_____

_____

_____

_____

_____

_____

_____

_____

_____

_____

_____

MY SOUL FINDS REST IN GOD ALONE; MY SALVATION COMES FROM HIM.

PSALM 62:1